ALL WAYS FAMILY

Books for Kids From the
American Psychological Association

Idea original: © Dexeus Mujer, 2018
Illustraciones: © Cristina Losantos, 2018
Texto: © Noemí Fernández, 2018
Asesoramiento científico: Pedro N. Barri, Montserrat Boada,
Buenaventura Coroleu, Sofía Fournier, Alberto Rodríguez-Melcón,
Bernat Serra

© Editorial Planeta, S. A., 2018
Avda. Diagonal, 662-664, 08034 Barcelona (España)
www.planetadelibrosinfantilyjuvenil.com
www.planetadelibros.com

Illustraciones del mural: Ignacio Ventura, Inés Ventura, Julio Barri,
Mariona Lora-Tamayo, Patrícia Lora-Tamayo

Primera ediciòn: marzo de 2018 ISBN: 978-84-08-18324-2
Legal Deposit: B. 2.666-2018 Impreso en España

Magination Press is a registered trademark of the American
Psychological Association. Order books at maginationpress.org,
or call 1-800-374-2721.

Book design by Gwen Grafft
Printed by Worzalla, Stevens Point, WI

Library of Congress Cataloging-in-Publication Datais on file
with the Library of Congress.

LCN: 2019017911
ISBN: 9781433831522

Manufactured in the United States of America
10 9 8 7 6 5 4 3 2 1

ALL WAYS FAMILY

Noemí Fernández Selva • Cristina Losantos

Magination Press • Washington, DC
American Psychological Assocation

ALL WAYS FAMILY

Riiiiinggg!
It's time for school.

Paula is excited this morning. She can't sit still or concentrate during class.

"Paula, what is fifty plus fifty?" Ms. Williams asks her.

"Um… Three hundred?" Paula answers.

Ms. Williams shakes her head. "What's up? You're a little distracted and not really paying attention."

"My parents are picking me up today. We're going to the doctor because my mom is pregnant. I get to see my little brother for the first time."

"Congratulations, Paula!" Ms. Williams says. "Now I understand why you're so distracted! Maybe you can tell us all about it tomorrow."

Paula's parents are waiting by the door when school ends.

"Mom! Dad! You're here!"

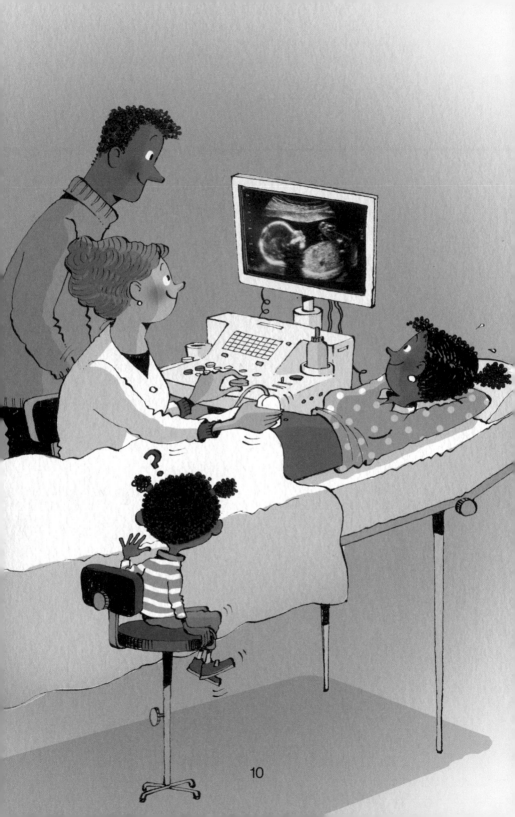

When they enter the OB/GYN office, Dr. Mills greets them.

"Good afternoon, Paula. Do you want to see your little brother?"

Dr. Mills takes them into a small room with an ultrasound machine, a device used to see the inside of a person's body.

"How are you feeling?" Dr. Mills asks Mom. "You are at 20 weeks."

"I'm fine!" Mom lays on the exam table next to the ultrasound machine and lifts her shirt. Dr. Mills dims the lights and spreads a clear gel below Mom's belly button.

"Oh! It's cold!" says Mom, winking at Paula.

Dr. Mills slides the ultrasound probe over Mom's belly. Fuzzy white, grey, and black images appear on the screen.

"Let's look at the size of the femur…Perfect! I see little feet and hands," she continues to move the probe over Mom's belly. "The heart is beating strong! Do you want to hear it?"

Dr. Mills presses a button and a fast, loud *bumbump bumbump bumbump* fills the room. Everyone smiles at each other, listening to the sound.

Paula stares at the screen.

"What is that?"

"Here's your brother's head and his chest," Dr. Mills points at the screen. "I'll print out the ultrasound image. It's called a sonogram. You can show it to your friends, Paula."

The next day at school, Paula brings the sonogram to class.

"Look at my little brother!" Paula exclaims.

"That's so cool, Paula! Wow!" Martina says.

"Dr. Mills gave it to me so I could show you. It's like a photograph of the inside of my Mom's belly. You can see my baby brother. Here's his head and this is his chest." Paula uses her finger to trace the outline of her brother.

"Ah, I see him now!" Sarah cries out.

"Ok, class, let's have a seat," says Ms. Williams. She asks Paula for the sonogram and explains the process of reproduction and fertilization.

"A baby develops during a long process that begins when a sperm cell joins an ovum," she says.

"So, we all come from sperm and an ovum?" asks Sarah.

"Yes, that's how babies begin. Isn't that amazing?" asks Ms. Williams.

REPRODUCTION & PREGNANCY

Babies are made by a process called reproduction. Sexual intercourse is a common form of reproduction. Reproduction begins when a sperm cell joins, or fertilizes, an ovum. A sperm cell and an ovum are called gametes. A person can produce an ovum, a sperm, or neither. Typically, a female adolescent or adult can produce an ovum and a male adolescent or adult can produce a sperm.

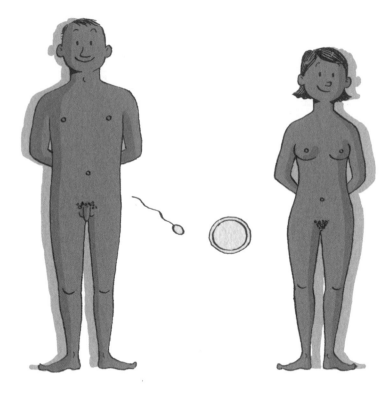

When sperm enters an adolescent or adult female's body, it goes into the fallopian tubes (these are reproductive organs inside of a female body) and waits until the ovum is released from the ovary.

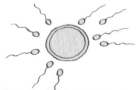

Millions of sperm release, but only about 40 make it to the fallopian tubes. The ovum opens itself and allows one sperm in.

Once the head of the sperm is completely inside the ovum, a new cell is created called the zygote. The zygote begins to divide into a ball of many, many cells. It moves to the uterus, which takes a few days, to implant in the lining of the uterus.

After the zygote grows more, the cells are called an embryo. It will start to receive nutrients and oxygen from the pregnant person by an umbilical cord. The embryo will continue dividing and growing. After eight weeks the embryo is called a fetus.

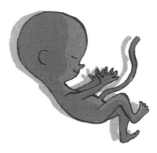

THE NINE MONTHS OF PREGNANCY

Week 6 (a month and a half):
The embryo is as small as a pea.

Week 8 (two months):
The embryo is the size of an olive! Nose, eyes, and ears have begun to form. After Week 8, the embryo is called a fetus.

Week 13 (three months):
The fetus is the size of a plum and is developing arms, legs, hands, feet, and fingers.

Week 17 (four months):
Now the fetus is the size of an avocado and Mom is beginning to develop a little bulge in her tummy. With an ultrasound, it might be possible to see if the fetus is a boy or a girl. The fetus also has toenails!

Week 22 (five months):
Now the fetus is the size of a banana and all of its organs are formed. It opens and closes its hands and sometimes grabs the umbilical cord.

Week 26 (six months): The fetus grows and grows! Now it's the size of a zucchini. Mom can feel the fetus because it moves a lot, and its little kicks are strong!

Week 29 (seven months): When the fetus reaches the size of a small pumpkin, it can recognize the voice of its mother, has eyelashes, and blinks.

Week 34 (eight months): The fetus has hair on its head, fingernails, and bulges out like a pineapple! Mom's getting tired and her tummy looks very large, but it's just her uterus and the fetus getting bigger.

Week 39 (nine months): The fetus is as big as a watermelon and is ready to be born!

When Martina gets home, her mother is waiting for her with a snack.

"I'm not very hungry, Mom," she says.

"Is something bothering you?"

"Paula brought a sonogram of her little brother today and the teacher explained to us how babies are made. So, if I don't have a father, how could I have been born?"

"Not all families—and moms or dads—become families in the same way. I went to the clinic where Dr. James works and they helped me give birth to you through assisted reproduction."

"What...?" said Martina.

"What do you say we go visit Dr. James?" said Mom. "I'm sure he can explain whatever you want to know."

"Your mother underwent a process that is known as assisted reproduction. There are many types, such as intrauterine insemination (IUI), in vitro fertilization (IVF), and introcytoplasmic sperm injection (ICSI). During IUI, we take sperm and inject it directly into the uterus so the sperm can fertilize an ovum within the body. IVF and ICSI requires us to take the ovum out of the body before putting it in contact with sperm in our laboratory. Your mom used IVF to get pregnant with you."

"But whose sperm fertilized Mom's ovum?" Martina asks.

"It came from a male adult who donated sperm to a sperm bank so that people who need it, like your mother, can get pregnant. Let's go to the lab and I can show you how assisted reproduction works."

ASSISTED REPRODUCTION:
IN VITRO FERTIZILATION (IVF)

Doctors can help all
types of people have a
baby through assisted
reproduction.

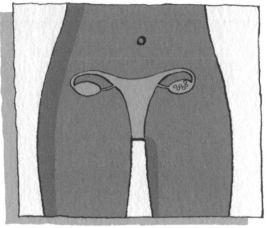

STIMULATION AND REMOVAL

For a period of 8 to 12 days, fertility drugs help produce
several ova that could be fertilized by sperm cells. When
the ova are ready, minor surgery is performed to carefully
remove the ova.

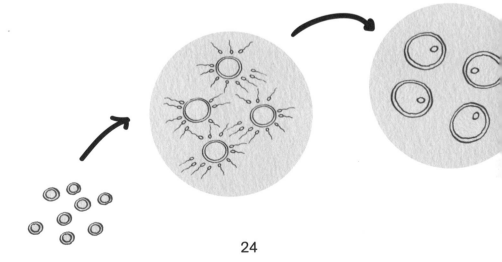

LABORATORY

In the laboratory, the medical technicians put each ovum in contact with thousands of sperm cells in hopes that a single sperm will fertilize an ovum.

When a sperm cell joins with an ovum, it is called fertilization. Because this happens in the lab, it is called in vitro fertilization or IVF.

If successful, an embryo develops, which is then kept for a few days in an incubator to mimic a person's body.

TRANSFER

Next, doctors place the embryos inside the uterus where it implants in the uterine lining and eventually develops into a fetus. In 40 weeks, a baby is born!

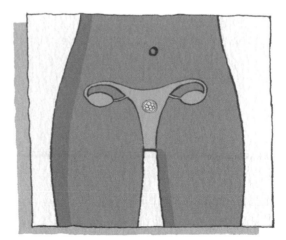

Dr. James gives Martina a lab suit, a pair of booties, and a hair cap. "Put these on over your clothes. You have to wear them to enter the assisted reproduction lab."

Martina enters the lab and sits on a stool in front of a computer. The technician explains to her another fertilization technique called intracytoplasmic sperm injection (ICSI).

"I'm going to show you how an ovum is fertilized with the help of a very small pipette. I never get tired of watching this process."

Martina stares at the screen and a large, round ovum appears before her eyes.

"Inside the pipette are sperm cells," the technician explains. "Now I will carefully insert it into the ovum…That's it! The ovum is now fertilized! Isn't it incredible? If you put your eyes up to the lens," she says, "you'll see an embryo from an ICSI we made a few days ago."

"It's so amazing!" says Martina.

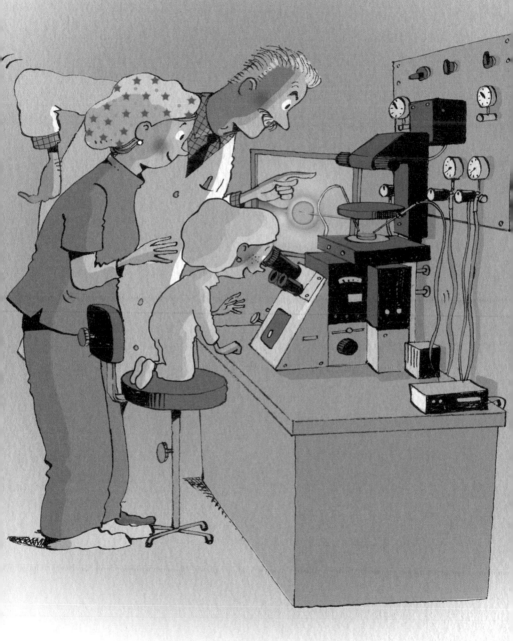

WHO DOES ASSISTED REPRODUCTION?

A female adult without a male partner who wants to be a parent might use assisted reproduction. Also, some people who want to have a baby using a surrogate have the option to use assisted reproduction.

Couples who cannot have children due to medical or health reasons may choose to use this method.

Lesbian couples (couples made up of two women) and gay couples (couples made up of two men) may choose to use assisted reproduction. They may use a sperm bank to fertilize an ovum or a surrogate to carry a child.

Couples may choose assisted reproduction because one or both members have a genetic disease they do not want transmitted to their child.

The technician takes Martina to the room where the frozen embryos, ova, and sperm are kept.

"If a female adult cannot use their own ova to get pregnant," Dr. James explains, "we can help by using donated ova. We store them in this tank. It is a type of freezer that is kept super cold: 320 degrees below zero! The ova are preserved here until they can be fertilized. The same goes for sperm. The embryos made by IVF or ICSI treatments that have not yet been implanted are also frozen here."

"Thanks for bringing me here, Mom! I learned all kinds of cool stuff!"

At recess, Martina explains everything she learned at the clinic.

"And you could see a real embryo?" asks Arnold.

"The real thing! My mom's doctor showed it to me under the microscope. It was an embryo they kept in an incubator, and the doctors will put it in a uterus, where it can grow into a baby. That's how I was born!"

"Oh, so that explains it!" exclaims Claire.

Ms. Williams overhears their conversation. "I think I know what we're going to talk about back in class," she says to herself with a smile.

In the classroom, Ms. Williams says, "Families are like people. They're all different and can be built in many ways. Just a few examples are:

Two-parent families where two adults who are a couple have children.

Single-parent families where there is only one parent.

Blended families, made up of two people who previously had children with someone else and now join together to form a new family.

Adoptive families, created when a couple or a single adult decides to adopt a child who is not their biological child.

Families without children, made up of two people who do not have children, either because they have not wanted to or because they have not been able to.

People can also be included in more than one family."

After this lesson, John is eager to explain what his family is like.

"When I was still a baby, my parents adopted me."

"So your mom didn't give birth to you?" Julia asks him.

"And your dad isn't your biological dad?" asks Paula.

"Right, I was born in another country!" John says.

"When I was born, my biological parents couldn't take care of me so I lived in an orphanage."

"I don't remember much because I was very young."

"My parents wanted to adopt a child and came to the orphanage to meet me!"

"As soon as they met me, we immediately began to love each other. I was very happy with them."

"When we arrived here, my grandparents, uncles, aunts, and cousins were waiting for us at the airport. Everyone was really looking forward to meeting me. And I wanted to meet them!"

WHO ADOPTS CHILDREN?

Couples who want to be parents but do not want to or cannot have children through assisted or unassisted reproduction can adopt children.

Couples who do not want to use assisted reproduction techniques and want to be parents may also adopt children.

People who do not have a partner and want to create a single-parent family often adopt children.

Couples who already have biological children may also decide to adopt children.

"Let's make a mural using everything we learned about families," Ms. Williams suggests.

"Can I paint my little brother inside my mother's belly?" asks Paula.

"And can I draw my mom's doctor in the lab?" shouts Martina.

"Of course!" Ms. Williams says. "When we're done, we can hang it up in the school hallway for everyone to see your family and ALL the ways you can be a family!"

"We know each other much better because we learned about each other's family," says Martina.

"Everyone has a different story," says Paula.

"There are so many ways to be a family," says John.

"What do you say we throw a party to celebrate all the different ways families are made!" suggests Ms. Williams.

What a great party!

FREQUENTLY ASKED QUESTIONS

My mom is pregnant. Is it normal for her body to change shape?

It's totally normal. Inside her uterus, the fetus grows day by day, gaining weight and volume. So your mom's uterus will grow bigger and rounder. Her body can also change in other ways.

Do all children have belly buttons, regardless of how we are conceived? What is the umbilical cord?

Every child and every adult has a belly button. When we are growing inside a person's uterus, we are still attached to them by the umbilical cord. This cord comes out of the navel and is a kind of tube through which the fetus receives the oxygen and nutrients it needs to develop. The umbilical cord is cut at birth because the baby can breathe and feed through its own mouth.

I'm expecting a little sibling. Will my parents stop loving me?

When a new member of the family arrives it is ok to have some doubts or feel a little fear over whether you will receive the same attention as before or if your parents will spend as much time with you. However, the love that parents have for their children never diminishes. It grows and grows all the time!

The moment a younger sibling arrives, parents will need to devote more time and attention to them because they can't do many things on their own. Since you're older, you can definitely help them!

Why are my friends' families different from mine?

Each family situation fits the circumstances of the people who are part of it. That's why we say there are different kinds of family.

Why are some children adopted and others not?

Sometimes the parents of a child cannot take care of them (because they are sick, they don't have enough resources, or they live in circumstances where it isn't easy to be a parent). They decide to find parents in another family through adoption who can care for the child as they grow up. This doesn't mean their biological parent(s) don't love them, just that they know there are other people who will be able to attend to their needs much better.

Are the people who have donated ova and sperm also parents of these children?

Ovum and sperm donors help other people who cannot have children and who choose assisted reproduction to become parents.

Although they are the ones who have biologically made the birth of the baby possible, they are often not part of the child's life.

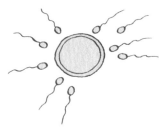

GLOSSARY

ADOPTIVE FAMILIES: Families made up of a couple or single adult who decide to raise a child that is not their biological child.

ASSISTED REPRODUCTION: A medical procedure where an ovum is removed from one person's body and sperm is removed from another person's body and the two are put in contact to create an embryo. The embryo is then placed inside the uterus. Assisted Reproduction includes both in vitro fertilization (IVF) and intracytoplasmic sperm injection (ICSI).

BLENDED FAMILIES: Families made up of two people who previously had children with someone else and now join together to form a new family.

EMBRYO: The embryo is made of many cells originally developed from a zygote.

FALLOPIAN TUBES: Reproductive organs in the female body that connect the ovaries to the uterus.

FAMILIES WITHOUT CHILDREN: Families that are made up of two or more people who are either not able to have children or choose not to have children.

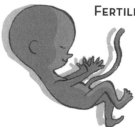

FERTILIZATION: The process by which an ovum and sperm join together to form a zygote that will develop into an embryo.

FETUS: The embryo is called a fetus after eight weeks of pregnancy until the baby is born.

GAMETE: Another name for a sperm cell or an ovum that is able to join for fertilization. Typically, a male adolescent or adult will produce sperm and a female adolescent or adult will produce ova, but this is not always the case. Some people produce neither.

GAY MAN: This is a person who identifies as a man who is primarily romantically and sexually attracted to other men.

INCUBATOR: A device used in assisted reproduction laboratories to grow embryos before they are transferred to the uterus. These devices maintain a temperature of 98.6° F and replicate the conditions of the uterus so the embryos can develop properly.

IN VITRO FERTILIZATION (IVF): Medical procedure where ova (removed from a person's body) are put in contact (in a laboratory) with sperm so that the sperm and ovum can join together to eventually form an embryo.

INTRACYTOPLASMIC SPERM INJECTION (ICSI): This is a medical procedure where ova are removed from the body and fertilized by a sperm in a laboratory using a pipette.

INTRAUTERINE INSEMINATION (IUI): This is a medical procedure where sperm is injected into a uterus to increase the chance of fertilization of an ovum.

LESBIAN: This is a person who identifies as a woman and who is primarily romantically and sexually attracted to other women.

MICROSCOPE: A tool used to view very small objects, such as an ovum or a sperm.

OB/GYN: A doctor who specializes in the health of female adolescents or adults and their reproductive organs: the uterus, vagina, ovaries, and ova. This doctor is also an expert in pregnancy and childbirth.

OVA: The plural form of ovum, the female reproductive cells.

OVARIES: These are female reproductive organs where ova are made.

OVUM: The ova are the female reproductive cells. They are produced by the ovaries in female adolescents and adults. One ovum is released every 28 days (approximately). If the ovum meets a sperm that is waiting in the fallopian tube, fertilization and pregnancy can occur.

PIPETTE: A delicate tool used in laboratories. Pipettes are used to collect ova and embryos.

PREGNANCY: This is when a female adolescent or adult has a developing zygote, embryo, or fetus in their uterus. It takes about nine months for the fetus to develop fully in the uterus.

REPRODUCTION: This is a process where a sperm cell joins an ovum and a pregnancy is possible; process in which individual offspring are produced.

SINGLE-PARENT FAMILIES: These are families made up of one parent with at least one child.

SONOGRAM: A visual image produced from an ultrasound exam.

SPERM: Sperm are male reproductive cells. They are produced by the testicles. If a sperm cell comes in contact with an ovum, it can ferilize it.

SPERM BANK: A place where sperm are stored from male adults who donate them so people can have children through assisted reproduction.

SURROGATE: A female adult who bears a child on behalf of another person, either using her own fertilized ovum, or from the implantation of another person's fertilized ovum.

TESTICLES: These are male reproductive organs where sperm are made.

TWO-PARENT FAMILIES: These are families made up of two adults who are a couple that have at least one child.

ULTRASOUND: A medical device that uses sound waves to view the organs inside the body. This device is very useful for monitoring the fetus during pregnancy, as it obtains different images, called sonograms.

UTERINE LINING (ENDOMETRIUM): The inner wall of the uterus where the embryo is implanted.

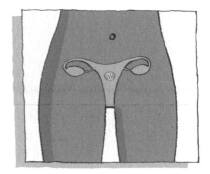

UTERUS: This is an organ located within the female body, which receives the fertilized ovum and nourishes it to grow during the nine months of pregnancy.

ZYGOTE: A single cell resulting from a fertilized ovum. It divides and becomes a ball of cells that implants in the lining of the uterus.

ABOUT THE AUTHOR AND ILLUSTRATOR

Noemí Fernández Selva is a teacher and a children's book author who has published books on emotions, values, and creativity. She lives in Barcelona. Visit noemifernandezselva.com.

Cristina Losantos has a degree in Fine Arts, worked as a teacher, and has published many popular children's books. She lives in Barcelona, Spain. Visit her on Instagram @cristina_losantos_sistach.

The renowned **Dexeus Mujer Women's Hospital** in Barcelona, Spain, specializes in gynecology, pregnancy, and assisted reproduction. The publication of this book was inspired by the many families that the staff cares for.

ABOUT MAGINATION PRESS

Magination Press is the children's book imprint of the American Psychological Association. Through APA's publications, the association shares with the world mental health expertise and psychological knowledge. Magination Press books reach young readers and their parents and caregivers to make navigating life's challenges a little easier. It's the combined power of psychology and literature that makes a Magination Press book special. Visit maginationpress.org.